Original title:
Blooming Byways

Copyright © 2025 Creative Arts Management OÜ
All rights reserved.

Author: Simon Fairchild
ISBN HARDBACK: 978-1-80567-007-0
ISBN PAPERBACK: 978-1-80567-087-2

## **Whispers of Wildflowers**

In fields where daisies dance and twirl,
A bumblebee took a fateful swirl.
He tripped on petals, oh what a scene,
Buzzing loudly, as if he were seen!

The poppies giggled, the tulips sighed,
"Did you see that? He nearly fried!"
But Mr. Bee just shook his head,
And hid away in a flowerbed.

## Serendipity in Sunlight

A dandelion wished to fly high,
But sneezed so loud, painted the sky!
"Oh dear!" it said, as feathers flew,
"Next time, I'll plan this rendezvous."

Sunlight laughed, tickling the grass,
"Let's not be too hasty, my friend, alas!
For every sneeze that sets you free,
There's always pollen to disagree!"

## Trails of Unfolding Dreams

A caterpillar dreamed of being bold,
But stumbled once on a marigold.
"Who knew this flower had such an edge?"
He blurted out from the safety ledge!

The blossoms rolled with laughter sweet,
"Come on, buddy, up on your feet!
Transform your dream; don't just sit tight,
Next time, jump off with all your might!"

## Vibrant Echoes of the Meadow

In meadows where the butterflies boast,
A ladybug claimed, "I'm the host!"
But lost her way in a tall green grass,
"Is this my party? Am I an ass?"

Crickets chirped, with a giggling tone,
"Don't worry, dear! You are not alone!"
"Just twist and turn, you're almost there,
And don't forget the disco flair!"

**Petal-Flecked Memories**

In the garden of giggles, things are bright,
Bees dance like they've lost all their flight.
Sunflowers wear hats, looking quite grand,
While daisies tell stories, oh isn't it bland?

Pigeons throw parties, they coo and they strut,
While squirrels debate on who knows the best nut.
Butterflies flutter, with a wink and a tease,
And frogs sing karaoke—man, how they please!

## Meadowlark's Reverie

A lark settles down on a fence made of dreams,
Tripping on daisies, or so it seems.
With a flip of its tail, it starts to croon,
While ants in a line march to a strange tune.

The grass asks the daisies, 'Where's the next dance?'
While crickets in tuxes take skillful stance.
A ladybug laughs, wearing polka-dot flair,
In the tale of the meadow, there's joy everywhere!

## Essence of the Unseen Trail

Amidst the tall grass, there's a rustling sound,
Is it a rabbit, or lost dreams that abound?
Mice wear capes made of fallen leaves bright,
While they plot to fly home under the moonlight.

The path bends and curves, oh what a delight,
With shadows that dance in the soft, fading light.
A weasel in sunglasses just can't keep still,
As he declares, 'I'm the king of this hill!'

## Radiant Footsteps in the Wilderness

Down the wild path, with laughter and cheer,
The racoons in masks host a party, oh dear!
With cupcakes made of bark, such a clever treat,
While owls in bow ties declare, 'Take a seat!'

The squirrels serve cocktails from acorn shells,
While frogs in tuxedos share tall, tall tales.
The night casts a spell, full of sparkles and winks,
Where every wild creature joins in and thinks!

## Stories Bursting with Color

In a land where laughter grows,
A squirrel wears mismatched clothes.
He juggles nuts and shimmies quick,
While painting trees in neon slick.

A parrot sings with silly tone,
It tried to carve its name in stone.
But slipped and fell right in the creek,
And splashed the crowd—it's quite the freak!

Flowers giggle at the sun,
Their petals dance, they love to run.
A bee joins in, a buzzing jest,
Who knew these blooms could be such pests?

So come and see this joyful spree,
Where chuckles bloom on every tree.
Let's laugh with critters, weird and bright,
In stories bursting with delight!

## Wonder beneath the Canopy

Underneath the leafy shade,
A turtle plays the ukulele.
He sings of bugs that dance and sway,
While squirrels cheer him on, hooray!

A raccoon tries to take a selfie,
But ends up with mud, it's kind of healthy.
He grins and squeaks, 'Look at this!'
As nature shares its wacky bliss.

The branches sway, a swing of fate,
An owl hoots, 'Let's celebrate!'
He throws a party in the night,
With fireflies glowing, what a sight!

So wander through this forest fun,
Where every moment's a playful pun.
Underneath the vast green dome,
You'll find your heart can truly roam!

## The Encounter of Sun and Soil

Beneath the sun, the soil cracks,
A worm wears shades and sunlit slacks.
With a wink, a seed starts to giggle,
As it rolls in earth, doing a little wiggle.

The sun shouts out, 'I'm here for a tan!'
Soil replies, 'For worms, I'm the biggest fan!'
Together they laugh, a comical sight,
Growing a garden from morning to night.

## Dances of the Floating Seeds

Dandelions float like tiny balloons,
Tickling noses and making tunes.
They swirl and twirl on a mischievous breeze,
Chasing each other like playful bees.

As they drift down, they scatter and land,
Thinking, 'Oh, wouldn't a garden be grand?'
With laughter they settle on curious ground,
Planning a party where flowers abound.

## Natural Cadence of Color

In the garden, colors collide,
Silly hues take a joyful ride.
Pink and yellow, then green and blue,
Each shade giggles, 'Look at me, too!'

The tulips dance with the daffodils,
While the roses trade their colorful frills.
'Let's paint the world,' they cheerfully chant,
'With splashes of laughter, it'll be quite a flaunt!'

## **Serenity Along the Symphony**

The grass whispers secrets to bees that hum,
While flowers join in, creating a drum.
A butterfly slips, does a little spin,
Over a daisy, wearing a grin.

Rippling leaves join in harmony,
Creating a tune that sets spirits free.
With each little note, joy starts to rise,
Nature's a riot, in clever disguise.

## A Tapestry of Life Unfurled

In the garden, gnomes play tricks,
Chasing squirrels, dodging sticks.
Tulips dance in polka dots,
While daisies argue about their spots.

Bees wear tiny hats and buzz,
Making honey, just because.
Ladybugs throw a fancy ball,
Where caterpillars crawl and crawl.

Sunshine tickles every leaf,
As birds debate who's the chief.
Petunias giggle, swaying free,
While weeds try to steal the spree.

Life's a show, such vibrant hues,
In costumes made of morning dew.
Each petal laughs as time unfurls,
In a garden full of whirling whirls.

## Nature's Whimsical Pathways

A rabbit wears a polka-dot tie,
While butterflies dance in the sky.
Tiny ants ride on flowers bold,
Trading stories, legends old.

The breeze plays peek-a-boo with trees,
As squirrels clown around with ease.
Every leaf a comedian bright,
Under the sun's warm, silly light.

Mushrooms hold a tea party grand,
With toadstools serving the best brand.
Grasshoppers sing in harmony,
As dandelions giggle with glee.

Every path tells a funny tale,
With flowers wearing tiny veils.
In this realm, joy skips and plays,
On nature's whims, through leafy bays.

## **Treading on Blossoming Trails**

Winding paths where daisies wink,
And every flower thrives on pink.
Porcupines wear shoes made of fluff,
While moonbeams whisper, "That's enough!"

Bumblebees having a fun race,
Over petals, each in their place.
Every fern has a slyly grin,
As butterflies twirl, spin, and spin.

Dandelion seeds float like dreams,
Tickling noses with silly beams.
Caterpillars joke about their weight,
As ladybugs plan a blind date.

Laughter echoes where colors thrive,
In nature's play, we feel alive.
Every hike is a comedy fest,
On trails where jesting blooms are dressed.

## The Language of Ferns and Flowers

Ferns discuss the latest news,
In fashion hues of vibrant blues.
Petals gossip with a sly wink,
Creating a buzz with every blink.

Cacti wear shades and soak in sun,
While sunflowers compete for fun.
Every cactus makes a pun,
Rattles shaking as they run.

The daisies try to tell a joke,
About a mushroom, quite the bloke.
Lavender giggles, 'What's the punch?'
As roses plan for the next lunch.

In this garden, laughter reigns,
Where every bloom has silly chains.
The language shared, a floral glee,
In nature's world, wild and free.

## Unexpected Sprouts of Hope

In cracks of sidewalk, bright flowers cheer,
They wave and dance, no sign of fear.
They greet the pigeons with laughter loud,
Making the mundane feel rather proud.

Between the cars, a dandelion grins,
Challenging asphalt with quirky spins.
Who knew such joy could bloom on streets?
A riot of colors where concrete meets!

Gardens of weeds, a sight so grand,
They plot their takeover, a stealthy band.
With petals like laughs that won't go away,
They'll turn your frown into a bouquet!

So next time you stumble upon some green,
Remember the party that's been unseen.
Nature's pranksters in shades of delight,
Sprouting smiles from morning till night.

## **Kindred Spirits of the Green Margins**

Snails wear top hats, they know how to dress,
Mice hold tea parties, just to impress.
Grassy patches, where misfits convene,
Plotting their schemes, oh what a scene!

A ladybug waltzes on blades of lawn,
While a caterpillar croons an old song.
Nature's mischief, in every nook,
Finding joy in every cranny and crook.

Twirling petals spin yarns of delight,
As bees crack jokes under soft moonlight.
The worms are the critics, they always tease,
Swaying along with the thumping breeze.

Raise a toast to these green and odd mates,
In their little world, oh how they celebrate!
With laughter like blossoms, they twine and twirl,
Kindred spirits, in a leafy whirl.

**Tapestry of Grass and Stone**

Pebbles chuckle in the midday sun,
As blades of grass play hide and run.
Together they weave a tale so bright,
Creating a patchwork of pure delight.

Moss joins the party, a fuzzy delight,
Whispering secrets in the soft moonlight.
Crickets strum tunes on a stick and a stone,
While nature's oddities practice their tone.

Forget-me-nots giggle, teasing the bees,
Who bumble around with utmost unease.
Each root winks at travelers rushing by,
Weaving a spell with their joyous sigh.

Dandelions poke out their heads in glee,
Declaring, "Hey, won't you come dance with me?"
A light-hearted gala, on paths they trod,
This tapestry hums with the love of the odd.

## An Ode to the Unseen Gardens

Behind every fence lies a secret lair,
Where fluffballs frolic without a care.
Squirrels don capes, the heroes of fun,
In unseen gardens where mischief's begun.

Bees hold debates on the best way to land,
While hidden gnomes work on their band.
With umbrellas of petals, they sway to the beat,
Hosting a festival that's quite the treat!

Invisible fairies concoct bubble tea,
As laughter erupts from a tall maple tree.
Wildflowers whisper the verses of cheer,
Inviting all wanderers to stop and steer.

So tiptoe beyond where the eye doesn't see,
Join the rascals for a cup of sweet glee.
In these unseen gardens, joy is the prize,
Where every blink opens a new surprise.

## Curves of Color in the Landscape

In fields of yellow, cows play hopscotch,
While daisies whisper, "We'll never botch!"
The sun is winking, oh what a sight,
As a lilac tells jokes to a bush of white.

A butterfly flutters, wearing a tie,
"Look at me dance!" it shouts, flying high,
The tulips giggle, swaying with flair,
"We bloom in style; come join us, if you dare!"

## Fragrance of Freedom

The roses are plotting a fragrant spree,
Inviting the bees for a wild jubilee!
Lavender's dancing, it's quite a scene,
Reminding the daisies they need some caffeine.

In the garden, a gopher plays the flute,
While sunflowers cheer, "We're ready for loot!"
Petunias are twirling, bumping a beat,
As geraniums join in, tapping their feet!

## **Enchanted Routes of Renewal**

On twisting trails, mushrooms wear caps,
And giggly ferns share their comical raps.
A dandelion shouts, "I'm still in my prime!"
As the buttercups hum a tune out of time.

Somewhere in the bushes, a squirrel breaks dance,
While ivy sticks close, saying, "Take a chance!"
The clouds roll in, play hide and seek,
As flowers chuckle, "Wow, aren't we unique?"

## **Serenity in Floral Whispers**

Petals exchange secrets in breezy chats,
"Who wore it better, me or the acrobatic bats?"
Butterflies gossip in soft, gentle tones,
While fungi make plans to throw fancy loans.

Amidst the laughter, a bee spins a tale,
Of sweet nectar races over the vale.
The daisies decide to start a book club,
"Let's meet at dawn, and care not for the grub!"

## Nature's Brushstrokes in Motion

In the park, a squirrel dances,
Laughing at its own romancing.
A butterfly steals a tasty snack,
While the flowers giggle, 'Watch your back!'

The bees hold an afternoon spree,
Buzzing loud in nonsensical glee.
A ladybug winks, feeling quite grand,
As ants march by in a conga line band.

The grass tickles toes, a plush delight,
While pinecones plot mischief, oh what a sight!
Petunias gossip, they can't be shy,
While daisies roll their eyes, oh my!

With each step taken, surprises unfurl,
Nature's antics make the heart twirl.
A dance of delight, all colors shine,
In this lively world, everything's fine!

## The Garden's Hidden Secrets

In a patch where gnomes like to sing,
Pansies plot a hidden thing.
A cabbage whispers secrets untold,
While the marigolds blush, oh so bold!

Worms have a meeting, so discreet,
Discussing the tastiness of roots to eat.
A frog in a hat croaks a new tune,
While herbs laugh at their own green boon!

The daisies play cards, what a sight,
While violets argue who's more polite.
A moth with glasses reads a book,
Insects gather 'round, take a look!

Petals giggle, pulling pranks,
As snails give their slimy thanks.
In this garden of playful delight,
The hidden adventures make day turn to night!

## Strolls Through Emerald Stories

On a path where wildflowers weave,
A rabbit tells tales that weaves and leaves.
With every hop, he plants a pun,
While daisies laugh in the warm, bright sun.

A curious deer peeks through the green,
Wonders what's happening, oh what a scene!
Cardinals chime in, a merry band,
With jokes that make nature's heart expand.

A rusty bike tire brings back a tale,
Of a raccoon who tried to set sail.
Over hills, through dales, and past the brook,
All the critters give him a quizzical look!

In emerald hues, stories unfold,
Nature's laughter is pure as gold.
Every stroll, a new chapter calls,
In this realm where whimsy enthralls!

## Canopies of Color

Beneath the trees, a painter's dream,
Splashes of color bursting at the seam.
The ferns in a flirt ruffle with grace,
While bushes giggle, they can't keep pace!

A peacock struts, flaunting each hue,
As chicks crack jokes, oh if they only knew!
Colorful petals are all in a fuss,
While the lilacs tease, 'You're missing the bus!'

Sunlight filters, a playful dance,
While shadows play hide and seek at a glance.
Trees wear hats made of twinkling leaves,
Whispering secrets the daylight weaves.

In canopies thick, with a jolly cheer,
Nature's color scape is drawing near.
Join the fun, in this vibrant spree,
Where every hue tells a tale of glee!

## **Sun-Kissed Wanderings**

The sun sat high, a giant dime,
Chasing shadows in a silly rhyme.
A squirrel danced, quite out of tune,
As butterflies held a wild cartoon.

With each step, our laughter soared,
Through fields where silly daisies roared.
We tripped on roots, fell into grace,
And tickled cacti in a wild race.

Mismatched socks in the open air,
Wearing hats shaped like a pear.
The road curved like a teasing snake,
In this world, a merry mistake.

At dusk, we toasted to the fun,
With mugs of juice, we'd finally run.
To capture joy, our fancy scheme,
A laugh, a giggle—a sunny dream.

## Captured in Petal Light

Petals whisper tales of glee,
As bees wear hats like they're at sea.
Roses giggle; tulips nap,
While daisies plot a bouncy trap.

A ladybug with a tiny grin,
Winks at the blooms, let the fun begin.
Sunlight dances on each leaf,
A comedy of nature, beyond belief.

We played tag with the fleeting breeze,
Tripping over whims like clumsy peas.
Petals caught laughter without a care,
"We're flowers!" they sang, "who needs a chair?"

As stars peeked through in the twilight's dress,
Nature's laughter echoed, oh what a mess!
With petals swaying, we danced in delight,
Captured forever in this petal light.

## Chasing Soft Horizons

Horizons soft like marshmallow fluff,
Tease our senses; oh, that's quite enough!
With each step, we'd twist and twirl,
Chasing giggles as hopes unfurl.

The clouds above play peek-a-boo,
As skaters swish with a happy crew.
We slipped on dreams, just like on ice,
Giggles burst forth; oh, what a slice!

The sun threw paint across the sky,
As if it laughed with a gentle sigh.
We cartwheeled under the cotton candy light,
Chasing colors as day turned to night.

With pockets full of fluffy clouds,
We spun in circles, oh how it loud!
In this chase, we found our way,
Soft horizons made a silly play.

## Harmonies of the Hued Horizon

Colors sing in a high-pitched tune,
A rainbow band beneath the moon.
Jellybeans tumble down the lane,
With gummy bears dancing in the rain.

Painted skies and whispered dreams,
As laughter echoes in turbo streams.
We twist and twirl through fields of cheer,
Silly giggles ringing loud and clear.

A green grass band plays hide and seek,
While flowers dance, all cheek to cheek.
The horizon glows in festive wear,
In harmonies, we shriek, we dare!

At day's end, we catch our breath,
In hues that tease the sleeping earth.
With silly songs that echo through,
We bid farewell to the vibrant view.

## The Colorful Veins of Forgotten Roads

Lost socks tango in the breeze,
While gumdrops dance on rusty knees.
A snail in shades of neon green,
Claims the pavement, quite a scene.

Dandelions wave to passing cars,
As squirrels mime their acrobats afar.
With every step, the laughter grows,
Who knew roads could wear such clothes?

Traffic cones seem to join the play,
They're doing yoga every day.
And potholes turn to little ponds,
Where rubber ducks make their absconds.

So let's forget the racing grind,
In every crack, fun's easy to find.
Together, let's embrace the quirky,
Those paths less traveled, oh so jerky!

## Flora's Gentle Embrace in the City

Petunias peek from cocktail cups,
While bees wear hats, like tiny pups.
In places loud, a soft wink flies,
As ivy creeps, giving high fives.

Cacti sport their prickly suits,
While lilies gossip in sharp toots.
Sunset blushes, all aglow,
As city folks join the flower show.

Bananas slip on sidewalk seams,
While daisies whisper silly dreams.
Between honks and hurried sales,
Nature's pulse hilariously prevails.

So grab your shades and join the fun,
We'll dance with petals in the sun.
In this wild, vibrant, leafy spree,
Who knew city life held such glee?

## Hidden Gardens Between the Cracks

Crackled pavements hide little sprites,
Who trade for snacks and giggle at nights.
A daisy dons a tiny crown,
While ants parade like a circus town.

Raccoons in tuxedos, classy crew,
Throw parties in the moonlight dew.
Their woodland plans, a masquerade,
In alleyways, a grand charade.

With each step, a treasure found,
A marigold grows in the ground.
And ladybugs with little bags,
Chat with pigeons in soft rags.

Nature whispers through cement cracks,
Laughter echoes, no time for lacks.
In this playful urban spree,
The best of gardens surely be!

## Nature's Canvas on Concrete

The city streets wear splashes bright,
With paint from flowers in playful flight.
A sunflower scrawls a happy face,
As puddles reflect a silly space.

Graffiti vines climb way up high,
While squirrels pose like models shy.
They strut and flaunt their fluffy tails,
In this concrete jungle, humor prevails.

Lettuce lounges on a public bench,
While broccoli takes a daring clench.
Street signs jam with croaking frogs,
Singing songs with circling dogs.

Every crack's a whimsical tale,
Where laughter lifts and worries pale.
Artful nature holds the key,
To a world that's wild, bright, and free!

## **Petals Beneath the Pavement**

Beneath the cracks, a flower grins,
Claiming space where no life wins.
A daisy cracks a joke so bright,
'Who needs a garden? I've got streetlight!'

A buttercup joins the fun parade,
With a dance and sway, no need for shade.
She shouts, 'Hey, folks, don't walk so fast!
I'm here to party, let's make it last!'

## Whispers of the Wildflower Path

On the edge of sidewalks, whispers float,
'Why do bees buzz? They think they're haute!'
A tulip blushes, adorned in style,
Making ants dance in a fashionable file.

A daffodil snickers, tip-toeing near,
'You'd think these roots have nothing to fear!'
But clovers giggle, they know it's true,
Life's quite the laugh when you're growing askew!

## Sun-Kissed Trails of Tenderness

Under the sun, a sunflower beams,
Dreaming of days that burst with schemes.
'Why walk in line when you can prance?
Come join my dance, let's skip the trance!'

A rose chimes in, with petals so grand,
'Life's just a joke, don't take it too bland!'
Together they twirl on the warm, soft earth,
Bringing laughter to spring's cheerful birth.

## Secret Blooms in Urban Corners

In a hidden nook, a secret smiles,
A violet peeks out, with charming wiles.
'You thought I'd fade? Hold your applause,
I've got roots that defy all your laws!'

A chic little fern flips her leaves with glee,
'Just because you can't see me, doesn't mean I'm free!'
Together they giggle, in a city's embrace,
Finding wild joy in the smallest of space.

## The Illumination of Wandering

In a land where sneakers squeak,
And every sign shows what to seek,
I tripped on roots and laughed aloud,
Was just a flower hiding, proud.

Over hills and valleys I danced,
With squirrels who simply took a chance,
They winked at me, oh what a prank,
As I fell, then got up with a plank.

Bumblebees buzzed a silly song,
They gathered nectar all day long,
I joined their dance, but lost my hat,
A bee now wears it, how 'bout that?

In shadows, gnomes play peek-a-boo,
With mushrooms giving a friendly cue,
I skipped along, embracing the jest,
A clumsy traveler on a flower quest.

## Nature's Whispering Path

On a trail where whispers squeak,
Each leaf as loud as a rubber beak,
I wandered, giggling, no doubt,
Stumbling over sticks, shouting out.

The trees had faces, oh what fun,
With bushy beards, they'd surely run,
Yet as I turned to take a look,
They froze like statues in a book.

A rabbit raced by with a sneeze,
Chasing butterflies like a tease,
In their flight, I felt quite grand,
Till a bee collided, oh the stand!

Silly squirrels threw acorns down,
As I danced in my floppy crown,
Nature chuckled at my grand show,
A whimsical tale where laughter flows.

## **Petaled Passageways**

Through petaled paths of pure delight,
Wandering rabbits hop in flight,
Each flower grins, a silly face,
Inviting me to join the race.

I twirled with daisies, full of cheer,
A butterfly buzzed, 'Come over here!'
But I tripped on a root, oh dear me,
The flowers laughed, 'What a sight to see!'

Sunlight played tag on my nose,
Everywhere, a tickle from a rose,
With giggles shared among the blooms,
I felt at home in nature's rooms.

In this garden of joyful glee,
Bouncing bees sang just for me,
As petals danced upon the breeze,
I joined the fun, oh how to please!

## Driftwood and Daffodils

By the river where daffodils smile,
I found driftwood that traveled a mile,
It wobbled, it wiggled, and turned,
With stories of waves, oh how I yearned.

The sun winked down, a bright old friend,
As I built a throne for flowers to tend,
Crowned with reeds and a feathered hat,
The wind roared laughter, how about that?

A fish leaped high with a splashy shout,
It swam in circles, dancing about,
And I clomped my boots with joyful might,
While daisies cheered for the silly sight.

With driftwood secrets and blooms galore,
Nature's laughter echoed on the shore,
In this world where fun never stills,
Daffodils bloom and my heart fulfills.

## Secrets Beneath the Verdant Canopy

In the forest where squirrels dance,
A raccoon stole my sandwich by chance.
He grinned with joy, not a worry in sight,
While I stood there, laughing at this funny plight.

Leaves whisper tales, slightly askew,
Of a bear who tried fitting in a shoe.
The tree trunks giggle, swaying in glee,
As the critters engage in their own jubilee.

Mushrooms form circles in awkward charm,
While a rabbit tries yoga, it's pure alarm!
The canopy shrouds with a glimmering wink,
Nature's sneaky secrets make me rethink.

In shadows of green, mischief is rife,
Even the bushes are plotting with life.
So skip through the leaves, let your laughter fly,
For secrets are hidden, just take a sly spy.

## Flora's Gentle Embrace

Daisies prance under a sunny parade,
While butterflies practice their fluttering trade.
A bee accidentally bumped his head,
If flowers could giggle, they'd laugh instead!

Petals wear hats, or is that their style?
Violets give daisies a peek and a smile.
The roses are gossiping, oh how they tease,
'When did lilies start taking selfies with bees?'

In the meadow, a fox had a fumble,
He tripped on a daisy, went tumbling in jumbles.
Yet spring's gentle vibes keep us all in cheer,
Even when chaos brings everyone near.

With laughter and colors, the day slips away,
Flora's embrace makes us want to stay.
So wander through gardens, let joy take the lead,
For nature's a laugh that we all really need.

## **Footprints in Fragrant Fields**

In fields of gold, where the daisies sway,
I followed a squirrel who led me astray.
He dashed past a patch of bright marigolds,
And I tripped in laughter, my humor unfolds.

A snail's on a mission, slow as a tune,
While bees are arm wrestling under the moon.
The earth smells like cookies, so sweet and so grand,
I'm pretty sure nature has a whole baking band!

Footprints of frogs hop in zigzagged delight,
As crickets play music to liven the night.
Even a butterfly thinks he can sing,
While all of the flowers just twirl and swing.

These fragrant fields hide giggles galore,
In nature's embrace, there's always much more.
So dance through the petals and sing with the breeze,
For laughter's the treasure that springtime leaves.

## Sunlit Trails of Inspiration

On trails adorned with daisies so bright,
A hedgehog rolled by, quite a comical sight.
He peeked through the grass, a curious chap,
While I nearly stumbled, caught in my map.

The sunbeams tickle and dance on my face,
The chirping of crickets sets quite the pace.
A ladybug stumbled on eco-ballet,
As I chuckled along, feeling light as a feather.

On paths lined with laughter and wild daffodils,
An ant had a party, mounting great hills.
He shouted, 'Come join, it's a hoot and a half!'
Nature's own comic, stirring up laughs.

These sunlit trails lead to mirth and delight,
With each tiny creature stealing the night.
So skip down the paths, let your spirit ignite,
For life is a comedy bathed in pure light.

## Stories Written in Greenery

In the garden, squirrels chatter,
Plotting schemes of nuts and pitter-patter.
A rogue raccoon dons a hat so spry,
Sipping dew like it's a fancy pie.

The daisies gossip, swaying with glee,
While butterflies giggle, carefree and free.
A snail in a hurry, what a sight to see,
Sprints by a slowpoke—oh, woe is he!

Bumblebees breakdance on petals' stage,
Every bloom's a backdrop for their hilarious rage.
The ants march in ranks, but they trip on the way,
A parade of chaos, in disarray.

Amid the laughter, the sun wears a grin,
As pollen floats on, where the fun begins.
In this wild laughter, nature's no bore,
With each rustle and giggle, there's always more.

## Echoes of the Flowered Veil

Woken up by a croak, a frog's morning yell,
In the garden's vast green, it's a loud, hoppy swell.
"Time to jump higher!" it seems to declare,
While flowers giggle and flounce through the air.

The tulips tell tales of lovers long gone,
Wrapped in their petals like a snuggly dawn.
A dandelion poof floats, right into a sneeze,
Sending bees buzzing, all giggly with ease.

With petals like confetti, the blooms throw a bash,
While crickets tune up for a musical clash.
The mint leaves compete in a fragrant parade,
Challenging thyme to a scented charade.

At dusk, fireflies spark like tiny bright sparks,
As laughter erupts from the evening's remarks.
In this wild spectacle, life dances in style,
With echoes of nature, each second worthwhile.

## Sunrise Over Hidden Canopies

The sun cracks a joke as it peeks through the trees,
While squirrels gather berries, on a giggling spree.
A raccoon in jammies steals breakfast on box,
Wearing the sun's rays like some brilliant socks.

The leaves shimmy about, in a cheerful sway,
Tickling the branches throughout the long day.
A snail takes a selfie, a foot in each shot,
"Look at me, world! I'm the snail of the lot!"

Beneath the canopy, shadows dance low,
While beetles and bunnies break into a show.
The morning dew chuckles, a giggle or two,
As ants hold auditions for a circus debut.

As the sun dips low and the skies are aglow,
Nature wraps its hands 'round the funny, you know.
In the laughter of branches, the whispers so free,
The forest is a stage, and we all want to be.

## Canvassed Dreams Under the Sky

A painter appears, with colors so bright,
Splashing joy on the canvas of day and night.
The clouds throw a party, spinning in white,
While shrubs shake their leaves, with sheer delight.

Daisies wear crowns, in ridiculous flair,
While roses strike poses, showing off their hair.
A ladybug waltzes, twirling with grace,
In this lively ballet, all things find their place.

A breeze takes a breath and whispers a tune,
As petals all nod like they're caught in a swoon.
The sun winks at shadows, and giggles dance by,
Creating a moment that never says goodbye.

With laughter in colors and joy all around,
Nature's a playground, delightful and sound.
In this vivid dreamscape, we all are a part,
Canvas of funny, painted with heart.

## Twilight's Blooms by the Narrow Lane

In twilight's grip, we stroll along,
Where flowers giggle, life feels strong.
A daffodil whispers, 'Who am I?'
While tulips chuckle, oh my, oh my!

Honeybees dance with a boisterous flair,
Waving at passersby without a care.
A sunflower tips its hat so grand,
As daisies form a hilarious band!

Above, the clouds toss shades of blue,
While prankster rivers play peek-a-boo.
'Look at me,' the petals shout with glee,
As petals plot mischief, oh can't you see?

With each soft breeze, the laughter sways,
As nature plays tricks in splendid ways.
So join the fun, don't hide away,
In this narrow lane where joys at play!

## **Colors of the Contemplative Walk**

Strolling through colors, bright as a meme,
Leaves whisper secrets, a shared dream.
A rose winks, says, 'Look at my hue,'
While violets giggle, 'Yes, we knew!'

The grass rustles, like gossiping friends,
In this joyful place where laughter blends.
'What's your shade today?' asks the tree,
As clouds roll in, shaping silly glee.

Petunias prance, in their playful attire,
Cracking jokes like a comedic flyer.
A peony exclaims, 'I'm the star!'
While lilies hide, saying, 'Not from afar!'

This walk is something, can't help but grin,
With pals that chirp and blossoms that spin.
In these vivid hues, let spirits be free,
On this stroll, forever, just you and me!

## The Sweet Gaze of Nature's Reclamation

In the garden wild, laughter takes flight,
As weeds wear crowns, feeling just right.
A clover giggles, 'I'm rare and proud,'
While dandelions cheer, drawing a crowd!

Petals and thorns, an odd couple's jest,
Who knew nature was so uninterested?
Bramble bushes share punchlines with glee,
While a squirrel laughs, 'Now that's a spree!'

Sunlight's a jester, casting long shadows,
While ants march on, like tiny gallows.
A flower sings high, 'Let's throw a bash!'
As bumblebees dance, zigzag and flash!

With every hue, giggles erupt,
In this reclaimed patch, joy's erupting sup.
So tip your hat to the blooming brigade,
Where laughter and nature, together are made!

## Urban Petals and Starlit Nights

In the concrete jungle, flowers take a stand,
Growing through cracks, isn't that grand?
'Look at me!' says a daisy so bright,
While city lights twinkle, oh what a sight!

Potholes become ponds for a daring sprout,
Hitching a ride on the subway route.
A lilac shouts, 'I'm sprucing this space,'
Turning dull sidewalks into a floral race!

Under starlit nights, petals sway and tease,
Dandelion wishes float on a breeze.
And a rose on the curb gives a cheeky wink,
As passersby pause, 'What do you think?'

With laughter and color, this urban delight,
Where petals and dreams dance under the night.
So join the fun in this floral spree,
In a city where whimsy is wild and free!

## Serendipity Along the Dusty Path

A squirrel wore a tiny hat,
While looking for a snack to chat.
He tripped on roots with quite a flair,
And landed in a garden chair.

A hedgehog sang a tune so bright,
His voice echoed in the daylight.
But bees buzzed in, they stole the show,
And danced around him to and fro.

The flowers laughed in hues so bold,
Whispering secrets, tales retold.
Each step revealed some silly sight,
Where laughter chased away the night.

So wander down this winding lane,
Where nature's humor's free of pain.
With every twist and turns to take,
A giggling bud will surely wake.

## Troubadours of the Wildflower Hour

In meadows bright, where daisies sing,
A rabbit pulls a tiny string.
He strummed a tune, oh what a show,
While flowers joined in, high and low.

The wind blew soft, a merry tease,
Tickling all the busy bees.
They spun around with lazy grace,
And dripped sweet nectar on their face.

The sun peeked in with a cheeky grin,
As butterflies danced with a spin.
They twirled in colors, bold and loud,
To woo the critters, gather a crowd.

So gather 'round this floral fable,
Where laughter blooms, if you're able.
The troubadours, they sing their part,
With every note, they share their heart.

## The Journey of a Fragile Stem

A tiny sprout with lots of dreams,
Set off one day down silver streams.
Each step was wobbly, oh so fun,
He giggled at the warming sun.

The ants, they marched in neat little rows,
But tripped on roots, struck funny poses.
While ladybugs were playing chess,
They argued loud, oh, what a mess!

With every stride, the world revealed,
A patch of soil where laughter healed.
A mushroom lamp, quite out of place,
Lit up the night with a quirky face.

So join the sprout in this wild dance,
Where giggles blossom, given a chance.
For every stem must find its light,
And journey forth with all its might.

## Petals on the Path

A flower fell, it twirled and spun,
Said, "Oops! I meant to be the one!"
It landed near a sleepy snail,
Who whispered secrets of the trail.

The grass began to sway and sway,
As crickets joined the pure ballet.
They chirped in beats and jumped in time,
Creating rhythms, oh so prime.

Then came a bee with a buzzing grin,
He claimed, "This party's where it's in!"
He jived around with silly flair,
As blossoms joined without a care.

So stroll along where petals lay,
And let your laughter light the way.
For every step on this bright track,
Will fill your heart and never lack.

## Hues of Harmony in Transition

A flower in a pot, so bold,
Wonders what the grass has told.
"I grow here, safe and snug," it sighs,
While outside, a bug simply flies.

The daisies danced in Sunday's breeze,
While tulips giggled with such ease.
"Watch me twirl!" one flower cried,
But tripped on roots and fell, oh my!

Petals paint the lanes with glee,
As squirrels scurry just to see.
They laugh at men who stop and stare,
"Why do they smell? What's with that hair?"

Daffodils plot a pranky game,
They bloom just high, then shout your name.
Catch them while they're in their prime,
Or risk a face-full of sunshine slime!

## Hidden Utopia of the Path

A squirrel with shades sits by a log,
Watching butterflies dance like a fog.
"What's that scent?" he winks with pride,
"Is it dinner or flowers?" he asks, bemused and wide.

The path ahead, a twisty surprise,
Where daisies plot to mesmerize.
Watch your step—it's quite absurd,
You'll slip and slide through a flying bird!

Cacti cracking jokes in the sun,
Pretend to frown, it's all in fun.
"Did you hear the rose and thorn debate?"
"Guess who won? We all can relate!"

Bumblebees buzzing, they hum and swoon,
As daisies sport their very best tune.
"Just swing with us!" the flowers beckon,
Tickling toes, that's their old weapon!

## Radiance Woven in Earth

A dandelion gave a sneeze,
Spraying wishes on the breeze.
"Catch them quick, or they're all gone,
Like socks that vanish at the dawn!"

Potatoes underground, living vast,
Wondering why they're not cast.
"I'd make quite the movie star,"
They think, "if only I weren't so far!"

"Under the soil, I'm quite the sight!"
Said a radish, hiding with delight.
Roots think they're whispers, soft and shy,
But when no one's looking, they dance awry!

Above, the daisies host a show,
And giggle as the wind starts to blow.
"Hold your hats, it's a flower fight!"
Yelled a daffodil with great delight.

**Fragrant Footfalls Under the Sky**


A muddy path where flowers play,
Invite the animals for a stay.
"Bring your jokes!" the lilies plea,
"We'll perfume the air with our spree!"

Ants in line have a grand retreat,
And trip on petals—what a treat!
"Marching band led by a fuzzball's tail,
It's whimsy, not war, that we unveil!"

Crickets chirp, composing a tune,
That turns the sun to a dancing boon.
"Let's sway and sway, friends, with flair!
Each note is a wiggle, let's not despair!"

Crashed into leaves under the sun,
Where wildflowers laugh, and it's all in fun.
"Next time, avoid that muddy patch,"
But no one listens, it's a crazy catch!

## Serenity Among the Urban Embers

In the chaos of horns and squeals,
A pigeon struts like it owns the wheels.
Caffeine fueled joggers dash with glee,
While dandelions whisper, "Look at me!"

Skyscrapers loom like giant clocks,
As squirrels plot while nibbling on socks.
Sidewalks sprawl, a feline's kingdom,
Where butterflies dance—no need for a hymn!

A hot dog rolls, a comical sight,
Chasing behind a dog, what a flight!
Neon signs flicker, the night is alive,
While daffodils giggle, they quietly thrive.

Amidst the clatter, peace finds a way,
In the oddest spots, flowers choose to play.
Life's a circus, a strange art,
Where even a weed can steal your heart.

## Wanderer's Heart Amidst Petal Fables

Underneath the bridge, dirt paths sway,
A snail hustles; it's on a gourmet tray.
With marshmallow clouds floating above,
A bee takes its coffee, quite the star of love!

In this alley, where laughter unfolds,
The roses gossip; the daisies tell bold.
Vases wear hats, quirky and tall,
While tulips argue, who's top of the hall!

Footprints with stories strut side by side,
To tune of grasshoppers playing their ride.
Each bend reveals a new quirky face,
Nature's a comedian, a verdant embrace.

With petals as pillows, dreams start to creep,
In this wanderer's heart, laughter runs deep.
Every turn, another oddity to find,
In this tale of colors, we're all intertwined.

## The Dance of Flora in the Urban Space

In crowded corners, colors collide,
Where sunflowers waltz in the great city ride.
Tangled in traffic, a rose strikes a pose,
While daisies twirl in their bright Sunday clothes.

A blender whirs; can you guess the sound?
It's the jungle's laughter, pure joy all around.
Pigeons practice their ballet above,
As ivy giggles, in shades of love.

Chasing the breeze, the daisies declare,
"We'll steal the show; come see if you dare!"
With a jig and a hop, forget the strife,
In sidewalks of chaos, they dance through life.

Sidewalk graffiti blends with flower art,
In the city square, every bloom plays a part.
Amidst the mayhem, a joyful embrace,
As petals chuckle in this lively space.

## Nature's Resilience in the Concrete Jungle

In cracks of pavement, life finds its voice,
With sprigs of green making a bold choice.
A lone daisy peeks from a guttered seam,
Whispering secrets, chasing a dream.

The sunflowers grin at the passing cars,
With roots entwined like rebellious stars.
Pavement cracks sing; it's a wild ballet,
Where weeds tell tales in a cheeky display.

A raccoon, tuxedoed, sneaks past the trash,
While daisies giggle; they flash and they splash.
In this concrete kingdom, laughter reigns bright,
As nature's champions dance into the night.

Each brick tells a story, each leaf a rhyme,
In this vibrant life where we twist with time.
Against all odds, joy takes its stance,
In a concrete jungle, we all find our dance.

## Colorful Calls of the Wild

In the woods, a squirrel chatters,
Wearing acorns like funny hats.
A bear waves with a honey stick,
Telling tales that make us laugh.

The birds have gathered, oh what a sight,
Singing songs of silly delights.
A rabbit hops in oversized shoes,
With a dance that banishes the blues.

The fox is busy, painting his tail,
With colors bright; he'll never fail.
He prances around, showing off style,
Even the trees can't help but smile.

Nature's circus, wild and free,
A playground for you and me.
In every nook, a giggle dwells,
Among the woods where laughter swells.

## Graffiti of Growth

On the alley walls, vines climb high,
With colors that nearly make you cry.
Graffiti flowers, wild and bold,
Tell stories of the young and old.

A sunflower smiles with a wink,
While daisies gossip, they love to think.
The cacti wear bright, paint-splashed shoes,
Giving life to the desolate views.

A ladybug finds a paintbrush too,
Creating spots of vibrant hue.
Butterflies flaunt their patterned wear,
As they float by without a care.

In this garden of art and glee,
Nature's canvas is wild and free.
Who knew growth could be so spry,
In this city where flowers fly?

## **Lace of Light Through Lilies**

Underneath the wavy reeds,
Where the light dances, nature leads.
A frog croaks jokes from a lily pad,
With a tongue-in-cheek that's oh so rad.

The dragonflies zip, a comedy show,
Sliding on water, putting on a flow.
Their wings shimmer, like quilted lace,
As they whirl around, keeping pace.

Turtles sunbathe with goofy grins,
While fish play tag and the fun begins.
Every splash invokes a delight,
Making ripples in pure sunlight.

We frolic where lilies swish and sway,
In this woven world of play.
Nature's laughter fills the air,
In this lake where joy is rare.

## **Enigmas of the Evergreen**

In the evergreen forest, secrets hide,
With pine-scented jokes that won't subside.
A wise old owl wears spectacles wide,
Chiming in with laughter, so dignified.

The trees dance awkwardly to play their tune,
Making shadows that seem to swoon.
A raccoon juggles acorns just for fun,
While pine cones giggle under the sun.

With squirrels plotting their nutty schemes,
And shadows playing tricks on our dreams,
Each rustle whispers tales to tell,
In this green world where humor dwells.

So prance with joy among the leaves,
Where every branch can tease and weave.
Nature's riddles make hearts skip,
In the evergreens, take a funny trip.

## The Melodies of Roots and Wings

In a garden of giggles, the flowers dance,
They sway on the breeze, as if in a trance.
A bee tried to sing, but stumbled, oh dear,
It buzzed to the rhythm of last summer's cheer.

The petals all chuckled at his clumsy tune,
They spun round the stem, saying, "We're in full bloom!"
With roots deep in laughter, they spread joy around,
Each dandelion wishes to tickle the ground.

At night, the crickets share tales with the sprout,
Of faraway places where they hop and shout.
A sunflower leaned in, with a wink and a grin,
"I've seen dapper rabbits dance with a chinchilla twin!"

So let's raise our glasses to nature's dear jest,
For in this wild world, we all play our quest.
With roots and with wings, we'll sing without care,
In the meadow of magic, let's all be aware!

## Lanterns of Lush Light

Under shade of tall trees, where shadows play tricks,
Mushrooms wear hats, and the toads teach us flips.
A lantern bug beams, it's the life of the night,
While owl hoots in rhythm, the spotlight feels right.

The ferns all are giggling, they toss and they twirl,
In a dance with the wind, they give life a whirl.
A squirrel in suspenders, with nuts by his side,
Is preparing a feast, oh what a grand ride!

Crickets wear tuxedos, with tails that fascinate,
And fireflies twinkle—oh, isn't it great?
In the glow of the moon, all life takes a seat,
For stories of mischief now echo the beat.

As laughter erupts from the heart of the glade,
It's clear that this frolic is nature's charade.
So come join the revelry, let's share in the cheer,
For tonight, dear friend, every creature is here!

## Artistic Paths of Petals

In gardens of chaos, the colors collide,
While tulips in top hats dance side by side.
With brushes of pollen, the bees start to paint,
Each flower a canvas, no need to complain.

Raindrops are laughter, they sprinkle the ground,
As vines twist and tangle, a stunt up and round.
A daisy declares, with a wink just for you,
"I always knew I'd be a star in this view!"

The roses all giggle in shades of pure pink,
While daisies compose, with no time to think.
On petals the snails leave behind little trails,
A map of their giggles, where wonder prevails.

With nature's own palette, we plot out our routes,
The paths through the petals, where joy is the truth.
So let's wear a smile, let our spirits soar high,
For the world is a canvas, let's splash, and let fly!

## **Thriving Through the Green**

In the thicket of fun, the critters convene,
A rabbit in sneakers leads quite the scene.
With carrots for maracas, they bounce with delight,
As the thumping of paws sets the party alight.

The hedgehogs have hats, and the owls are DJs,
They spin crazy tracks through the wild, leafy maze.
The daisies are rocking, in rhythm and time,
While the thyme plants hum along in sweet rhyme.

Up high in the canopy, chattering monkeys,
Drop down their banana peels, pure silence is funky.
The grasshoppers jitterbug, with twirls left and right,
While the flowers all join in the most epic flight.

So let's dance with the branches, let roots intertwine,
In this field of pure joy, every moment's divine.
With warmth in our hearts and laughter to share,
We thrive in the green, in this whimsical air!

# Tales from the Thicket

In the woods where squirrels chatter,
The bushes boast of gossip and chatter.
A raccoon wears a dapper hat,
While a hedgehog spills his tea — oh, what a spat!

A rabbit makes a fashion blunder,
Wearing carrots, what a wonder!
A snail races, but oh so slow,
While a bird just laughs, stealing the show!

With whispers of leaves, secrets flow,
As crickets recite tales, to and fro.
The thicket's a stage, all animals play,
In costumes of nature, they frolic and sway.

So if you wander through this lively place,
You might see a scene that brings a smile to your face.
Remember the antics of critters who roam,
The thicket's a circus that feels like home!

## The Orchestra of Natural Vistas

In the forest, the flutes start to squeak,
While the trees in concert begin to speak.
A trumpet blooms from a blossoming vine,
As a drummer beats on a log just in time!

A lark joins in with a high-pitched song,
While the bass of the river hums along.
The daisies sway as they dance in the breeze,
Their petals a waltz, such elegant tease!

The sunbeams shine like spotlights from above,
While insects tap dance on leaves, my love.
A butterfly flutters, the lead prima donna,
In this orchestra vast, nature's the subjona!

With willow bows and pine tree bows low,
The symphony thrives wherever you go.
So tune in your heart, let the laughter arise,
In this natural concert, joy wears no disguise!

## **Flutters of Wild Colors**

A canvas sprawls across the meadow,
With wild hues bursting, bright and yellow.
A bee in stripes thinks he's so fly,
While a ladybug winks as she zooms by!

The daisies giggle under the sun,
Their petals spin, just having fun.
A butterfly falls, doing a flip,
In a colorful swirl, it takes a quick trip!

The irises gossip in shades of blue,
Whispering secrets only flowers knew.
While poppies sway in splendid cheer,
Their party hats mock, "We're the ones here!"

So join this parade of colors so bright,
Where every bloom brings a chuckle and light.
In the gallery of nature, laughter unfolds,
With wild colors painting stories untold!

## Gentle Currents of Floral Essence

In the garden, the breezes tease,
Spreading scents that float with ease.
A daffodil plays a prank on a rose,
Trying to tickle her, oh, how it goes!

Lilies spin tales of sweet perfume,
To snatch a smile in their floral bloom.
A bumblebee laughs at a faux pas so grand,
As it dances clumsily, out of hand!

Petals flutter like giggles in the air,
As they gossip and twirl without a care.
The sunflowers nod, giving their advice,
While the daisies plan a surprise that's quite nice!

So stroll through the blooms, let laughter entwine,
With whispers of petals as soft as fine wine.
In these gentle currents, joy takes its chance,
And the garden invites all to dance!

## **Petal Trails of Quiet Reflections**

Butterflies in fancy shoes,
Dance on petals, so amused.
Bees with hats and stripes so neat,
Join the flowers for a treat.

Gossip blooms in colors bright,
Sunshine giggles, pure delight.
A daisy winks, a tulip laughs,
As silly squirrels steal the gaffs.

Hot air balloons float by in cheers,
Jellybeans fall, not fears.
A rainbow slides with sticky glee,
On a slide of honey tea.

The garden tosses confetti leaves,
As grasshoppers spin like thieves.
Underneath a laughing sky,
Nature hums a silly sigh.

## Where Weeds Whisper Secrets

In the corner, weeds conspire,
With secret tales that never tire.
They laugh and giggle, roots entwined,
Plotting pranks, the best designed.

A dandelion sings a tune,
To tickle bees that swoop and swoon.
They wear their pollen like a crown,
While ants parade in fields renowned.

Mirthful moles pop up for fun,
Declaring, 'We're all number one!'
They wear their hats made out of clay,
And dream of dancing through the day.

The whispers spin a tale so grand,
With glee that spreads across the land.
Where weeds and blooms both find their groove,
In laughter's song, they always move.

## Fields of Dreams on a Busy Street

Traffic stops for daisies bold,
While sunflowers twist to tales retold.
A ladybug rides the honk parade,
As petals pop in light cascade.

Sidewalks chatter with a trot,
Of city gardens, crazy plot.
With bright umbrellas sipping dew,
An artful scene, a vibrant view.

Pigeons strut with neighborly flair,
While chipmunks plot to steal the air.
The crosswalks dance, a flower show,
As laughter sparks from high to low.

Bumblebees wear tiny shades,
In fields of dreams where fun cascades.
With traffic lights that blink and tease,
Nature's sneak peek brings us ease.

## Roots Reaching for the Stratosphere

Rooted deep yet dreaming high,
Trees are wishing on the sky.
With arms stretched wide and leaves that sway,
They giggle at the clouds each day.

The carrots dance while underground,
Chanting tunes without a sound.
Potatoes joke of flying team,
While laughing in a veggie dream.

The sunbeams wink, the moonlight grins,
As roots scheme for their epic wins.
"Let's start a race to touch the stars,"
They chant as night begins to spar.

A thrilling ride on cosmic swings,
Where laughter blooms and joy still clings.
In this garden of acts so rare,
Roots reach high, while shadows share.

## Fragrant Echoes of the Wanderlust

I tripped on daisies, what a sight,
They giggled and danced, a pure delight.
A bee in a suit asked for a chat,
I said, "Not now, I'm busy with that!"

Running from shadows, I slipped on a shoe,
A rabbit was laughing, as they often do.
Chasing the scent of pies in the air,
I found a whole orchard; who knew it was there?

Snakes in the grass played a game of charades,
While squirrels debated the best nut parades.
Each step was a joke, each leaf a good laugh,
Nature's comedy club, what a fine staff!

With every misstep and stumble I take,
I laugh at the puddles, the jokes they can make.
So onward I wander, in giggles I roam,
The world's just a stage, each path is my home.

## **Blossoms in the Shade of Lanterns**

Under each lantern, the flowers conspire,
To throw a surprise, oh, ain't it a fire!
Petals like confetti, they dance in the breeze,
While beetles debate who should win the cheese.

A moth with a mustache struts down the lane,
While crickets all chorus, like they're in a train.
The hedges keep secrets, they snicker and grin,
As the night unfolds, let the silliness begin!

Bumblebees singing in harmony sweet,
Compete with the frogs, holding a feast.
I stumbled, I fumbled, my juice box did spill,
And the flowers all laughed, what a riotous thrill!

So tether your giggles, as lanterns light up,
With blossoms and laughter, let's fill up the cup.
In this shady escapade where fun never wanes,
We'll toast to the quirks, as the night still remains.

## Wild Wonders of the Sidewalks

On the cracked concrete, a flower stood tall,
Waving to pigeons, it had quite a call.
A snail in a shell wore a hat made of clay,
While ants formed a parade, oh, what a display!

A pinwheel was spinning, with gusto and flair,
While squirrels played poker, without any care.
With skips and with jumps, I joined the parade,
The stones were all laughing; could they be swayed?

Walking the wild paths, I spotted a shoe,
A lost and forlorn one, a tale it could brew.
I placed it on grass, where lost things all roam,
And watched as it giggled, found its way home!

Life on these sides, pure chaotic delight,
With wild wonders abound, every hour is bright.
So let's take a stroll, let's see what we find,
In grooves of the sidewalk, let fun unwind.

## Veils of Green Along the Pathway

Through veils of green, the path does invite,
Moss tickles toes; oh, what a delight!
A hedgehog with glasses is reading a book,
While tulips take selfies, with nary a look.

The ferns whisper secrets, they laugh as they sway,
I glanced at a snail, who's planning a play.
With mushrooms as seats, and grass for a stage,
These little green critters are full of great rage!

Daisies throwing parties, a bash for the ants,
With confetti of pollen, in wild, joyful chants.
I slipped on a leaf, took a tumble headlong,
While the lilacs all chuckled, to them it felt wrong!

Yet still, off I wander, with whimsy in tow,
In this green-swathed wonder, where laughter can flow.
Each step is a giggle; each turn, quite the jest,
In the veils of green, we are truly the best!

www.ingramcontent.com/pod-product-compliance
Lightning Source LLC
Chambersburg PA
CBHW072144200426
43209CB00051B/446